Allons-y!

Allo

Auteur général / D. Anthony Massey
Une expérience intégrale de communication en français
A complete communication experience in French

Répondez s'il vous plaît **1**

ns-y!

Catherine Bick
D. Anthony Massey
Denise Scuccato

Copp Clark Publishing
A division of Copp Clark Limited
Vancouver Calgary Toronto Montreal

ISBN 0 7730 1602 3

Edited by Danièle Caloz and Lidy Jarolimek

Design   /   Zena Denchik
Illustration   /   Sandy Glean, Wendy Morris,
         Judi Schachte, and Louise Wiatrowski
Cover Art   /   Sandy Glean, Wendy Morris, and
         Louise Wiatrowski

Copp Clark Publishing
517 Wellington Street West
Toronto, Ontario
M5V 1G1

Printed and bound in Canada

Table of contents

Meet the Latulipes

Meet the Poiriers

Meet the Lepages

Meet the Bonneaus

Meet Bélina, Picotin, and Zénon

unit 1

C'est un dentiste? Oh! la! la!

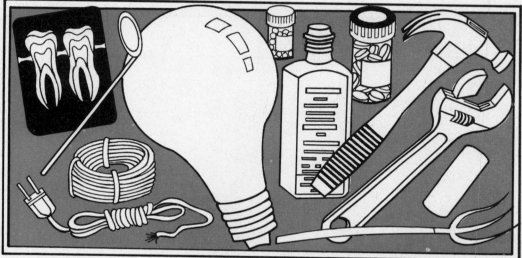

Let's learn it in French

When you have finished this unit, you will be able to:
- ask who someone is and introduce that person to a friend
- say hello and good-bye
- say the names of such occupations as: dentist, mechanic, druggist, farmer, electrician, and teacher
- read and write these new words and sentences
- say the numbers from zero to ten

The idea box

Bring the following to class:
- hats for a lady, a girl or a man
- pictures of a dentist, a mechanic, a druggist, a farmer, an electrician, a teacher, and of the tools that they use
- an illustrated magazine
- a telephone book

Language of your own

Situation 1 C'est Filou

Characters Rosalie, Jules, Francine, Nathalie, Filou
Setting The schoolyard
What happens The children are playing Blindman's Buff. Rosalie has a blindfold over her eyes. Filou touches her, but Rosalie does not recognize him. Finally, the dog barks and Rosalie cries, "Ah! c'est Filou!"

Situation 2   C'est un pharmacien

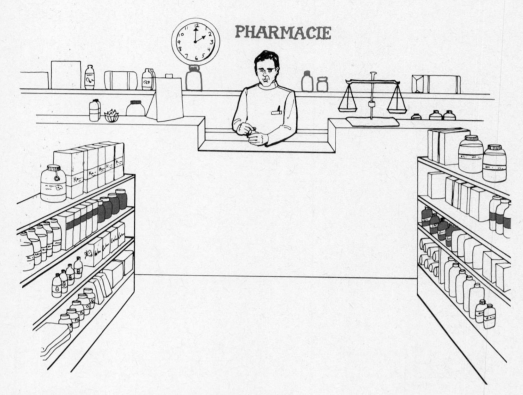

Characters   Marc, madame Bonneau
Setting   The drugstore
What happens   Marc thinks that the druggist he sees is a dentist.

Situation 3   C'est monsieur Dumas

Puppets   Picotin, Bélina
Props   A newspaper with a photograph of a man on the front page
What happens   Picotin picks up a newspaper and says that the picture he is looking at is that of monsieur Toc. Bélina looks at it and says that it is monsieur Tac. After a short argument, Bélina picks up the newspaper, reads slowly, and realizes that it is monsieur Dumas.

Chanson

(Mélodie: Chevaliers de la table ronde)

Refrain

Refrain

C'est un dentiste? Oui, oui, oui,
C'est un fermier? Non, non, non,
C'est un dentiste? Oui, c'est un dentiste.

1 Non, ce n'est pas un fermier,
  Non, non, non, ce n'est pas un fermier.

2 Non, ce n'est pas Picotin,
  Non, non, non, ce n'est pas Picotin.

1 Qui est-ce?
C'est Marc.

2 Qui est-ce?
C'est Jules.

3 Ce n'est pas Jojo;
c'est Nathalie.

4 Ce n'est pas Gigi;
c'est Filou.

5 C'est une dentiste.

6 6 C'est un mécanicien.

8 C'est un garçon.

7 Ce n'est pas un fermier.

9 C'est une fille.

unit 2

Regarde! Qu'est-ce que c'est?

Let's learn it in French

When you have finished this unit, you will be able to:
- say the names of some wild and domestic animals
- give commands such as, "Sit down!" "Stand up!" "Look!"
- ask another person's name and give your own name
- read and write these new words and sentences
- say the numbers from eleven to twenty

The idea box

Bring the following to class:
- a variety of toy animals
- pictures of animals (wild and domestic)
- a model farm or zoo

Situation 1   Au zoo

Characters   Nathalie, madame Lepage
Setting   The zoo
What happens   Nathalie upsets her mother by running from one animal to another, and asking all sorts of questions. Then, Nathalie and her mother stop in front of a wildcat.

Situation 2   A la ferme

Characters   Francine, Jules, monsieur Latulipe
Setting   The farmyard
What happens   Jules and Francine, accompanied by their father, visit their uncle's farm. The children easily recognize familiar animals such as chickens, cows, pigs. Then monsieur Latulipe shows Jules a duck and asks him what it is. Jules thinks at first that it is a turkey, but quickly realizes his mistake, while Francine makes fun of him.

Situation 3   Regarde, qu'est-ce que c'est?

Characters   Marc, Nathalie, Jojo, Rosalie
Setting   A classroom
What happens   On the desk is a picture of an imaginary animal. Jojo looks at the head and thinks it is an elephant. Marc looks at the tail and thinks it is a horse. Nathalie looks at the neck and thinks it is a giraffe. Clever Rosalie tries to please everyone by inventing a name, and the children are amused.

Chanson

(Mélodie: Old MacDonald had a farm)

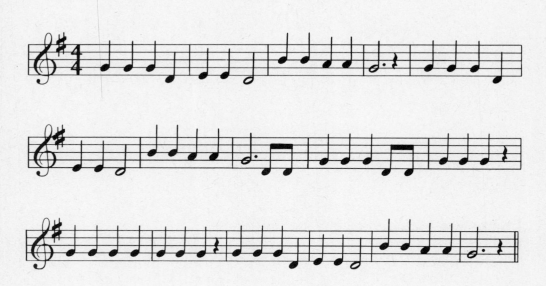

1 A la ferme de Zéphirin, i,a,i,a,o
   Il y a un tout petit chien, i,a,i,a,o
   Qui fait oua, oua, ci
   Qui fait oua, oua, là
   Oua, oua, ici, oua, oua là
   A la ferme de Zéphirin, i, a, i, a, o

2 A la ferme d'Archibald, i,a,i,a,o
   Il y a un gros cheval, i,a,i,a,o
   Qui fait ian, ci
   Qui fait ian, là
   Ian, ici, ian là
   A la ferme d'Archibald, i, a, i, a, o

Lecture 👓

1 Qu'est-ce que c'est?
C'est un chien.

4 Ce n'est pas une poule;
c'est un canard.

2 Qu'est-ce que c'est?
C'est une vache.

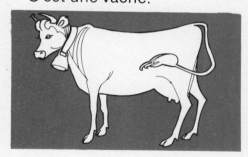

5 C'est un cochon.

3 Ce n'est pas un chat;
c'est un lion.

6 C'est une girafe.

Rouge ou bleu?

Let's learn it in French

When you have finished this unit, you will be able to:
- say the names of several colours and pieces of furniture
- ask questions about these colours and pieces of furniture
- give the names of a triangle, a circle, a square, and a rectangle
- read and write these new words and sentences

The idea box

Bring the following to class:
- a variety of coloured objects: books, pails, paintbrushes, pencils, toys
- colouring books
- coloured pictures of toys and animals

Situation 1 Quel désastre!

Characters Marc, Francine
Setting The Latulipes' home
What happens Francine is painting bookshelves. Marc, who is visiting, decides to help Francine and, while she is on the phone, he quickly paints four chairs. Francine is upset.

Situation 2 Donne-moi un crayon

Characters Jojo, Nathalie
Setting The Lepages' basement
What happens Nathalie slowly upsets her sister Jojo, first by bringing her a blue pencil instead of a red one, then by bothering her with questions about the colour of the pencils.

Situation 3 Ne regarde pas!

Puppets Zénon, Picotin
Props Flash cards of a yellow giraffe, a red truck, a blue ball, and a black dog
What happens After putting his toys in order, Zénon tries to make Picotin guess the colour of the blue ball, then of the red truck. Picotin guesses easily. Zénon then notices that Picotin is not holding his hands over his eyes.

(Mélodie: Le ciel est bleu)

1 C'est une chaise mauve?
Oui, c'est vrai.
C'est une chaise bleue?
Non, c'est faux.
C'est une chaise mauve,
Oui, c'est une chaise mauve.
C'est une chaise mauve?
Oui, c'est vrai.
C'est une chaise bleue?
Non, c'est faux.
C'est une chaise mauve.
C'est une chaise mauve.
C'est une chaise mauve.

2 C'est un lit rouge?
Oui, c'est vrai.
C'est un lit noir?
Non, c'est faux.
C'est un lit rouge,
Oui, c'est un lit rouge.
C'est un lit rouge?
Oui, c'est vrai.
C'est un lit noir?
Non, c'est faux.
C'est un lit rouge.
C'est un lit rouge.
C'est un lit rouge.

1 Ce n'est pas une chaise beige; c'est une chaise jaune.

2 C'est un crayon bleu.

3 Ce n'est pas un camion noir; c'est un camion rouge.

4 Ce n'est pas une balle mauve; c'est une balle jaune.

5 C'est une table orange; vrai ou faux? C'est vrai.

6 C'est un lit orange; vrai ou faux? C'est faux.

7 C'est un carré.

8 C'est un cercle.

Qu'est-ce qu'il y a dans le sac?

Let's learn it in French

When you have finished this unit, you will be able to:
- ask and tell what is in a box or a bag
- ask a person to find or to show you what is in a box or a bag
- read and write these new words and sentences
- add, using the numbers from one to twenty

The idea box

Bring the following to class:
- fruits and vegetables (real ones or pictures): potatoes, turnips, carrots, and cabbages
- flowers (real or artificial ones or pictures)
- an empty chocolate box, a paper bag, small toys or pictures of toys (a ball, a doll, a train)

Situation 1   Au marché

Characters   Jules
Setting   An open-air market
What happens   Jules is at the market. He is looking at each vegetable closely, but does not find what he wants. Fed up, the salesgirl points out a cabbage with a worm in it. Jules runs away and everyone laughs.

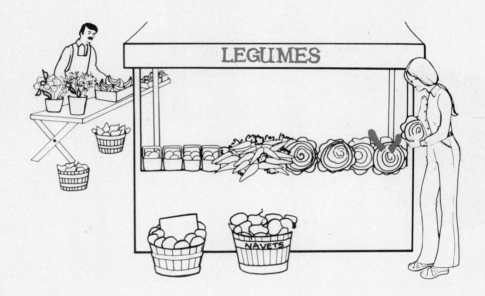

Situation 2   Quelle surprise!

Characters   The Latulipe family
Setting   The Latulipes' home
What happens   Monsieur Latulipe comes in carrying a box with chocolates in it for everyone. He hopes that the chocolates will be a surprise, but everyone ends up seeing them.

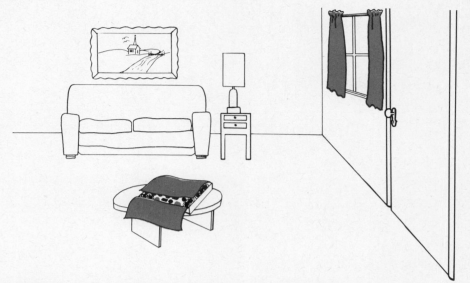

Situation 3   Qu'est-ce qu'il y a dans le sac?

Characters   Marc, madame Bonneau
Setting   Madame Bonneau's living-room
What happens   Madame Bonneau and three of her friends are playing bridge. Marc comes in with a bag and says that he has frogs in it. His mother tries to calm her guests, but Marc shows them the frogs. Angry, madame Bonneau chases Marc out of the living-room.

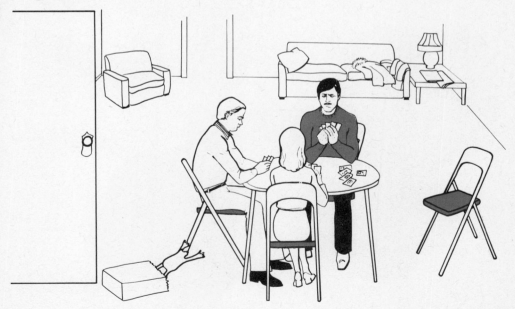

Chanson

(Mélodie: Mary had a little lamb)

1 Qu'est-ce qu'il y a dans la boîte?
   Dans la boîte, dans la boîte?
   Qu'est-ce qu'il y a dans la boîte?
   Oh! des chocolats.

2 Montre-moi un, deux, trois choux,
   Deux, trois choux, deux, trois choux,
   Montre-moi un, deux, trois choux,
   Là . . . Merci beaucoup.

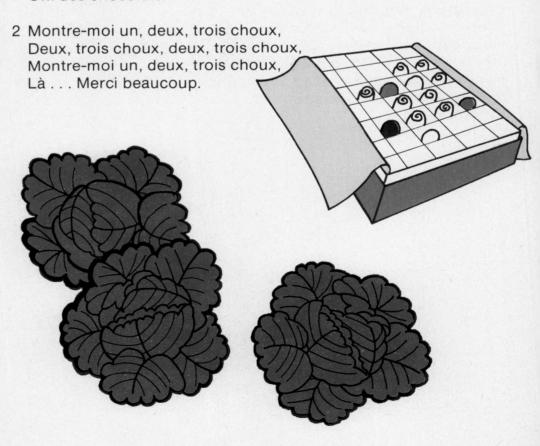

Lecture ••

1 Montre-moi des carottes.

2 Voilà des carottes.

3 Voilà une fleur.

4 Voilà des fleurs.

5 Voilà une pomme.

6 Voilà des pommes.

7 Qu'est-ce qu'il y a dans le sac?
Il y a des bananes dans le sac.

8 Qu'est-ce qu'il y a dans la boîte?
Il y a des navets dans la boîte.

1 Look at the sentences and listen to what your teacher reads. In your Activity Book: write the letter (a or b) of the sentence you hear.

Example:
a) C'est une boîte.
b) Voilà une boîte.
The teacher says: Voilà une boîte.

Answer b)

1 a) Voilà une fleur.
  b) Voilà des fleurs.

2 a) Qu'est-ce qu'il y a dans la boîte?
  b) Qu'est-ce qu'il y a dans le lit?

3 a) Montre-moi une carotte.
  b) Voilà une carotte.

4 a) Il y a des navets dans le sac.
  b) Il y a un navet dans le sac.

2 In your Activity Book: rewrite the sentences, replacing the words in colour with the words in brackets.

Example:
Il y a *une banane* dans la boîte.   (des balles)
Il y a des balles dans la boîte.

1 Qu'est-ce qu'il y a dans *le sac*?   (la boîte)
2 Il y a *une pomme* sur la boîte?   (des carottes)
3 Voilà *une fleur*   (des fleurs)
4 *Montre-moi* des carottes.   (Voilà)
5 Il y a *des balles* dans le sac?   (une pomme)

3 In your Activity Book: write five sentences. Use each word or phrase in a separate sentence.

1 Il y a   4 Voilà
2 Montre-moi   5 Qu'est-ce qu'il
3 des fleurs

C'est la balle de Filou

Let's learn it in French

When you have finished this unit, you will be able to:
- ask who owns something and say who owns something
- tell who owns and who does not own something
- say the names of several toys
- read and write these new words and sentences
- subtract, using the numbers from one to twenty

The idea box

Bring the following to class:
- balls of various sizes
- toys such as trains, rockets, sticks
- pencil cases, pens of various colours in their packages

Situation 1 A qui est la balle?

Characters Jules, Francine, Nathalie, Jojo, Filou
Setting The playground
What happens Jules and Francine find a ball. Jules thinks it is Jojo's ball; Francine thinks it is Nathalie's ball. But Jojo and Natha-lie, who are playing nearby, say that it is not their ball. Filou arrives and surprises everyone.

Situation 2 A qui est le bâton?

Puppets Zénon, Bélina
Props A train, a red rocket, a small stick with the name "Zénon" on it.
What happens Zénon is tidying up his toy-box and sees that most of the toys belong to Picotin. He thinks that the stick belongs to Picotin as well, but Bélina shows him the name "Zénon" written on it.

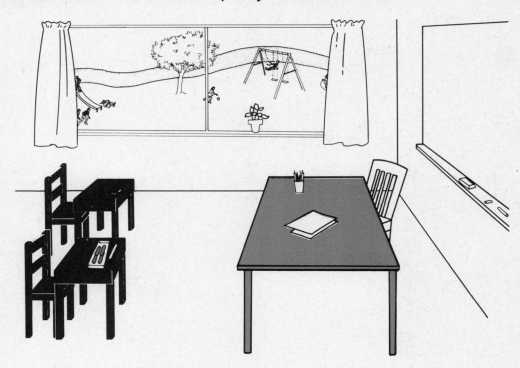

Characters Marc, Rosalie, Jojo
Setting The classroom
What happens Marc finds a box on Jojo's desk and asks what is in it. Rosalie, being clever, says that there are fountain-pens in it. Marc prefers the word "pen" and thinks that the word "fountain-pen" is very funny.

2 Look at the pictures and listen to the sentences. In your Activity
Book: write the letter of the sentence that matches each picture.

Example:

Listen:
a) C'est la balle de Nathalie.
b) C'est la balle de Filou.

Answer b)

Ecoute:

1

4

2

5

3

Chanson

(Mélodie: Sur le pont d'Avignon)

1 Sur le pont d'Avignon,
  C'est sa balle,
  C'n'est pas ma balle,
  Sur le pont d'Avignon,
  C'est la balle
  De Zénon.

2 Sur le pont d'Avignon,
  C'est son train,
  C'n'est pas mon train-ain,
  Sur le pont d'Avignon,
  C'est le train
  De Nathalie.

3 Sur le pont d'Avignon,
  C'est ses billes,
  C'n'est pas mes billes,
  Sur le pont d'Avignon,
  C'est les billes
  De Jojo.

1 C'est le bâton de Zénon;
   c'est son bâton.

4 A qui est la balle?
   C'est la balle de Filou?

2 C'est ta banane?
   Oui, c'est ma banane.

5 C'est mon train;
   c'est à moi.

3 C'est tes billes?
   Oui, c'est mes billes.

6 A qui est le stylo?
   C'est mon stylo.

1 Look at the sentences and listen to what your teacher reads. In your Activity Book: write the letter (a or b) of the sentence you hear.

Example:
a) C'est ta balle.
b) C'est ma balle.
The teacher says: C'est ta balle.
Answer a)

Ecoute:
1 a) C'est mon train.
　b) C'est son train.

2 a) C'est les poules de Bélina.
　b) C'est les balles de Bélina.

3 a) A qui est la balle?
　b) A qui est la bille?

4 a) C'est les trains de Zénon.
　b) C'est des trains de Zénon.

5 a) Voilà mon stylo.
　b) Voilà ton stylo.

2 In your Activity Book: rewrite the sentences, replacing the words in colour with the words in brackets.

Example:
C'est son *camion*.　(train)
C'est son train.

1 C'est *mon* train.　(ton)
2 C'est sa *fusée*.　(bille)
3 *C'est* les poules de Bélina.　(Voilà)
4 *C'est* les camions de Zénon.　(Regarde)
5 C'est à *moi*.　(toi)
6 Voilà les *billes* de Zénon.　(bâtons)
7 A qui est la *balle*?　(banane)
8 A qui est le *bâton*?　(lit)
9 C'est le *train* de Zénon.　(camion)
10 C'est *tes* balles.　(mes)

Donne-moi mon chapeau

Let's learn it in French

When you have finished this unit, you will be able to:
- ask where something is, tell where something is
- say the names of some furniture and clothing
- give simple orders
- read and write these new words and sentences

The idea box

Bring the following to class:
- a blouse, slippers, hats, real clothes, dolls' clothes or pictures of clothes

Language of your own

Situation 1 Où est ma blouse?

Characters Rosalie, madame Poirier
Setting The Poiriers' home
What happens Rosalie, always forgetful, looks everywhere for her blue blouse, first in her room, then in the living-room, where she finds in on a chair where she had left it.

Situation 2   Voilà tes pantoufles

Characters   The Latulipe family and Filou
Setting   The Latulipes' basement
What happens   Monsieur Latulipe is looking for his slippers and becomes more and more upset by the answers from various members of his family. Finally, Jules shows him Filou and, nearby, the chewed-up slippers.

Situation 3   C'est ton chapeau?

Puppets   Zénon, Picotin
Props   A new hat and an old hat, a chair, and a cushion
What happens   Picotin hides Zénon's hat under the cushion on the chair. Zénon sits down on it, when he comes in. When Zénon asks for his hat, Picotin pretends not to understand what is going on. Then he offers him an old hat. Finally, he tells him to get up. When he sees the joke that has been played on him, Zénon becomes angry and Picotin runs away.

Chanson

(Mélodie: Frère Jacques)

1 Mes pantoufles!   (2)
   Les voilà!   (2)

   Où sont mes pantoufles?   (2)
   Les voilà!   (2)

2 Ma chemise!   (2)
   La voilà!   (2)

   Où est ma chemise?   (2)
   La voilà!   (2)

1 Donne-moi mon chapeau.
   Voilà ton chapeau.

2 Où est le pantalon?
   Le pantalon est sur la chaise.

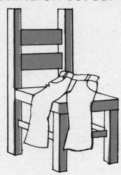

3 Où est ma blouse?
   Ta blouse est sur le lit.

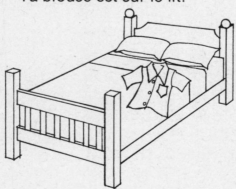

4 Où est la jupe de Bélina?
   La jupe de Bélina est sur le divan.

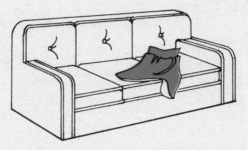

5 Où sont les pantoufles de Marc? Ses pantoufles sont dans le sac.

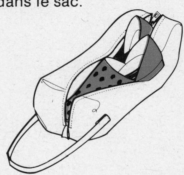

6 Où sont mes souliers?
   Tes souliers sont dans la boîte.

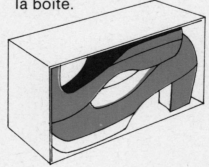

Exercices sur la lecture

1 Look at the sentences and listen to what your teacher reads. In your Activity Book: write the letter (a or b) of the sentence you hear.

1 a) Où est le pantalon?
  b) Où sont les pantalons?

2 a) Le pantalon est sur la boîte.
  b) Le pantalon est dans la boîte.

3 a) Donne-moi mes pantoufles.
  b) Donne-moi tes pantoufles.

4 a) Donne-moi mon chapeau.
  b) Donne-moi ton chapeau.

5 a) Où sont les pantoufles de Marc?
  b) Où sont tes pantoufles, Marc?

2 In your Activity Book: rewrite the sentences, replacing the words in colour with the words in brackets.

1 Où est *ma blouse*?   (mon pantalon)
2 Où sont *mes* souliers?   (tes)
3 Où est la *jupe* de Bélina?   (robe)
4 Voilà *un sac*.   (une boîte)
5 Mon pantalon est *sur* la boîte.   (dans)
6 *Ses* pantoufles sont dans le sac.   (Mes)
7 Tes souliers sont dans la *boîte*.   (commode)
8 Il y a *une jupe* dans la boîte.   (des jupes)
9 *Où sont* tes chemises?   (Voilà)
10 *Voilà* ma blouse.   (Donne-moi)

3 Read each reply and the following questions. In your Activity Book: write down the letter (a, b, or c) of the question that will give the reply.

1 Son pantalon est sur le lit.
  a) Où sont les pantalons, Marc?
  b) Où est le pantalon de Marc?
  c) Où est le lit de Marc?

36   2 La jupe de Bélina est sur le divan.
      a) Où sont les divans?
      b) Voilà la jupe.
      c) Où est la jupe de Bélina?

    3 Ses pantoufles sont dans le sac.
      a) Où est ma pantoufle?
      b) Où sont mes pantoufles?
      c) Où sont ses pantoufles?

    4 Tes souliers sont dans la boîte.
      a) Où sont mes souliers?
      b) Où est mon soulier?
      c) Où sont ses souliers?

    5 Ma blouse est sur la chaise.
      a) Voilà ta blouse.
      b) Où est ta blouse?
      c) Où est sa blouse?

unit 9

Il est drôle!

Let's learn it in French

When you have finished this unit, you will be able to:
- say what people do in a circus and whether or not they are funny
- say what you think about yourself and about others
- tell where people live and what their jobs are
- read and write these new words and sentences
- say the numbers from twenty to fifty

The idea box

- set up in your classroom a model circus with toy acrobats, jugglers, clowns, and animals. You can make use of toys, magazine pictures, dolls with costumes from other lands. You can also make paper figurines of circus characters and animals.

Situation 1   Bélina fait le clown

Puppets   Picotin, Bélina
What happens   Bélina wants to become an acrobat. She turns a somersault and falls. Picotin finds this very funny. Bélina then decides to be a clown.

Situation 2   Au cirque

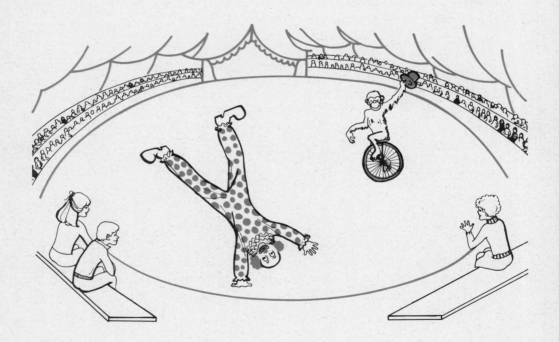

Characters   Rosalie, Marc
Setting   The circus tent
What happens   The circus is under way. Marc is laughing at the jokes of the monkey, but Rosalie finds him boring. Then the children watch a clown who is acting in a comical way in front of them. This time, Rosalie cannot stop herself and bursts out laughing.

Characters   Jules, Francine, monsieur Latulipe
Setting   Behind the Latulipes' house
What happens   Jules and Francine are arguing about who will be
the clown. Monsieur Latulipe hears the noise, comes out of the
house, slips, and falls. This makes the children laugh, but monsieur
Latulipe is angry.

1 Look at the pictures and listen to the sentences. In your Activity Book: write the letter of the sentence that matches each picture.

Ecoute:

1

2

3

4

5

3 If the sentence you hear matches the picture, say, "C'est vrai". If
the sentence you hear does not match the picture, say, "C'est
faux".

Ecoute:

Chanson

(Mélodie: Sur la route de Berthier)

Je suis clown et acrobate,
Je suis aussi magicien.
Regarde, je sors de la boîte,
Je suis aussi magicien.

Tu n'es pas clown,
Ni acrobate,
Tu n'es ni clown ni acrobate.

Je suis aussi magicien—cien—cien—cien
Ah! Je sors de la boîte, boîte
Je sors de la boîte, boîte
A surprise.

Lecture

1 Qui es-tu?
  Je suis Bélina.

2 Moi, je suis acrobate, et toi?
  Moi, je suis jongleur.

3 Il est magicien.

4 Elle est clown.

5 Je ne suis pas fâché.

6 Tu n'es pas drôle.

7 Il n'est pas jongleur.

8 Elle n'est pas acrobate.

1 In your Activity Book: write the letter (a, b or c) of the correct question for each reply your teacher gives you.

1 a) Qui est-ce?
  b) Tu es acrobate?
  c) Qu'est-ce que c'est?

2 a) Tu es clown?
  b) Elle est clown?
  c) Il est clown?

3 a) Je suis drôle?
  b) Tu es drôle?
  c) Il est drôle?

4 a) Tu es fâché?
  b) Il est fâché?
  c) Je suis fâché?

2 In your Activity Book: rewrite the sentences, replacing the words in colour with the words in brackets.

Example:
Je suis *clown*. (acrobate)
Je suis acrobate.

1 Je suis *jongleur*. (clown)
2 Tu es *drôle*. (fâché)
3 *Elle* est acrobate. (Il)
4 Il n'est pas *magicien*. (jongleur)
5 Je ne suis pas *fâché*. (drôle)

3 In your Activity Book: rewrite these sentences to give the opposite meaning.

Example:
Elle est professeur?
Non, elle n'est pas professeur.

1 Je suis drôle?
2 Il est magicien?
3 Elle est clown?
4 Tu es fâchée?
5 Je suis jongleur?

unit 10

Où est-ce?

Let's learn it in French

When you have finished this unit, you will be able to:
- ask and tell where things and people are
- read and write these new words and sentences
- ask and tell what the weather is like
- multiply with numbers from zero to fifty

The idea box

Bring the following to class:
- pictures of various buildings
- boxes of various sizes
- some candy
- pictures of various movie theatres, restaurants, and parks (you can also build these with construction paper)

Language of your own

Situation 1   Où est la balle de Nathalie?

Characters   Nathalie, monsieur Lepage
Setting   The Lepages' home
What happens   Monsieur Lepage is in the living-room. Nathalie comes in and asks where her ball is. Monsieur Lepage sends her outside, to the front and then to the back of the house. Nathalie does not find anything. Monsieur Lepage then realizes that the ball is right in front of him in the living-room.

Situation 2   Où est le bonbon?

Puppets   Zénon, Picotin
Props   A candy, a box, a table
What happens   Zénon is a magician who makes a candy disappear. Picotin knows where the candy is hidden, but pretends that he does not know.

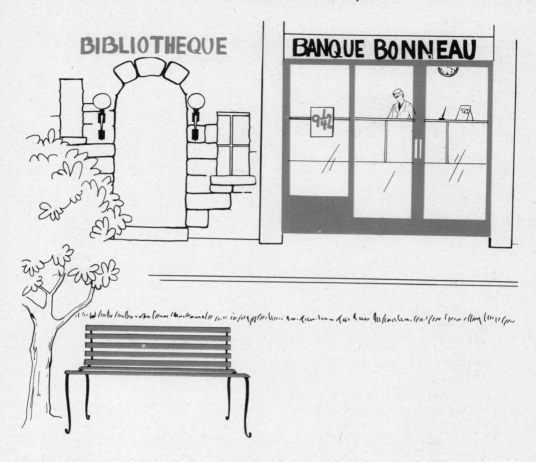

Characters   Francine, monsieur Lepage, madame Poirier
Setting   The street
What happens   Francine is looking for the bank. She asks monsieur Lepage where it is. He answers with a joke. Francine is angry and asks madame Poirier, who shows her that the bank is right in front of her.

2 Look at the pictures and listen to the sentences. In your Activity Book: write the letter of the sentence that matches each picture.

Example:

Listen:

Nathalie dit:
a) Où est ma balle?
b) Où est ta balle?

Answer a)

Ecoute:

1

4

2

5

3

6

Chanson

(Mélodie: Le p'tit cordonnier)

Papa, où est ma balle?
Ta balle est devant la maison.
Papa, où est ma balle?
Ta balle est derrière la maison.

Papa, voici ma balle,
La voici dans ma main!
Papa, voici ma balle,
Elle n'est pas au jardin!

1 Nathalie dit: "Je suis à la maison, je ne suis pas devant la maison."

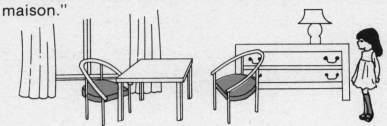

2 Bélina demande: "Où es-tu? Où es-tu, Zénon?"
Zénon répond: "Je suis derrière le divan."

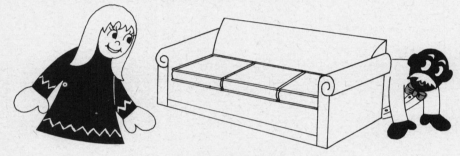

3 Tu n'es pas sous la chaise, tu es sur la chaise.

4 Francine est devant la banque.

5 Où est monsieur Lepage? Il n'est pas derrière la maison. Où est-il?

6 Où sont Jojo et Nathalie? Où sont-elles? Elles sont devant le restaurant.

7 Où sont Rosalie, Jules et Francine? Ils sont dehors.

8 Voilà le parc. Filou est au parc.

1 In your Activity Book: write the letter (a, b or c) of the sentence your teacher says.

1 a) Je suis sur la table.
   b) Je suis sous la table.
   c) Je suis devant la table.

2 a) Où es-tu?
   b) Où est-il?
   c) Où sont-elles?

3 a) Je ne suis pas au parc.
   b) Tu n'es pas au parc.
   c) Il n'est pas au parc.

4 a) Ils sont au restaurant.
   b) Elles sont au restaurant.
   c) Il est au restaurant.

5 a) Monsieur Lepage est devant le cinéma.
   b) Monsieur Lepage est derrière le cinéma.
   c) Monsieur Lepage n'est pas derrière le cinéma.

2 In your Activity Book: copy the question that gives the answer shown.

1 Ils sont devant la classe.
   a) Où est-il?
   b) Où sont-ils?
   c) Où sont-elles?

2 Oui, je suis derrière le cinéma.
   a) Tu es devant le cinéma?
   b) Je suis derrière le cinéma?
   c) Tu es derrière le cinéma?

3 Ils sont au restaurant.
   a) Où est Marc?
   b) Où sont Jojo et Nathalie?
   c) Où sont Jules et Francine?

4 Non, je ne suis pas dehors.
 a) Tu es dehors?
 b) Il n'est pas dehors?
 c) Je suis dehors?

5 Oui, il est sur la table.
 a) Nathalie est sur la table?
 b) Marc et Jojo sont sur la table?
 c) Marc est sur la table?

3 In your Activity Book: rewrite the sentences, replacing the words in colour with the words in brackets.

1 Il est *à* la maison.   (derrière)
2 *Elles* sont devant le restaurant.   (Ils)
3 Je suis devant *le cinéma*.   (le parc)
4 Ils ne sont pas *sur* la table.   (sous)
5 *Le chien* est sous le divan.   (Le chat)

Je n'ai pas de cheveux

Let's learn it in French

When you have finished this unit, you will be able to:
- say how people look
- say whether you are warm or cold
- read and write these new words and sentences
- ask and tell how many toys or other things people have

The idea box

Bring the following to class:
- toys, pictures or puppets representing people in various occupations
- toys or pictures representing Martians
- an envelope and a sheet of paper

Situation 1   C'est effrayant!

Characters   Jojo, Nathalie
Setting   The Lepages' basement
What happens   Nathalie and Jojo are watching television. Nathalie is scared by a picture of a very ugly Martian. Jojo comforts her.

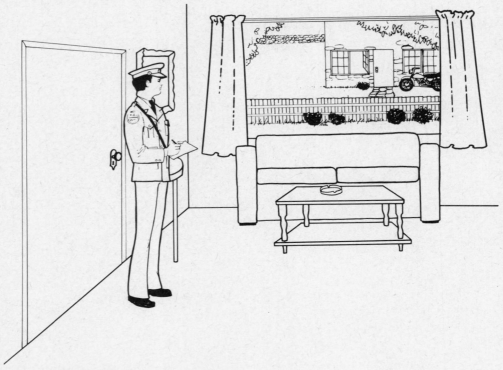

Characters Monsieur Lepage
Setting The Lepages' home
What happens One morning, monsieur Lepage is in the living-room looking out the window. He sees someone breaking into his neighbour's house. He calls the police. A policeman comes to get a description of the thief. The policeman quickly realizes that it is the neighbour's son, who does not have a key. Monsieur Lepage is embarrassed.

Situation 3   Une lettre

Puppets Zénon, Picotin
Props An envelope with a piece of paper in it
What happens Zénon is reading out loud a letter he has just written to a girl, in which he says how handsome he is. Picotin, who has come in quietly, hears this description and makes fun of his friend. Then he picks up the envelope to see the name of the girl. Zénon, who is angry, tries to catch Picotin, who runs away.

2 Look at the pictures and listen to the sentences. In your Activity Book: write the letter of the sentence that matches each picture.

Ecoute:

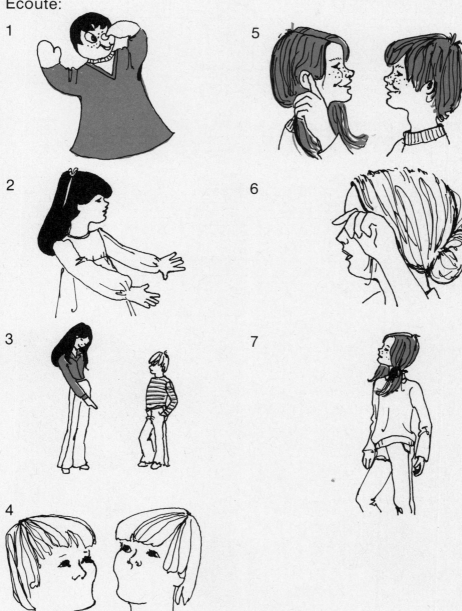

1

2

3

4

5

6

7

Chanson 🎵

(Mélodie: Cadet Rousselle)

J'ai un nez, deux yeux, une bouche,   (2)
Et toi, dis-moi, qu'est-ce que tu as?   (2)

Moi, j'ai une tête, mais pas de cheveux.   (2)

Ha, ha, ha, oui vraiment,
Ce que tu as l'air amusant!

1 Qu'est-ce que tu as sur la tête? J'ai des cheveux.

2 Le martien a un nez drôle; il n'a pas de bouche.

3 Ma poupée a des bras et des jambes.

4 Tu as une moustache? Non, je n'ai pas de moustache.

5 "Je n'ai pas de cheveux", dit Zénon.

6 Elles ont deux autos.

7 Ils n'ont pas d'auto.

1 In your Activity Book: copy the question that gives the answer shown.

1 J'ai une télévision.
  a) Qu'est-ce qu'il a?
  b) Qu'est-ce que tu as?
  c) Qu'est-ce que j'ai?

2 Non, il n'a pas de cheveux.
  a) Il a des cheveux?
  b) Tu as des cheveux?
  c) Qu'est-ce qu'il y a?

3 Elles ont des souliers.
  a) Qu'est-ce qu'il a?
  b) Qu'est-ce qu'elle a?
  c) Qu'est-ce qu'elles ont?

2 In your Activity Book: write four sentences. Use each word or phrase in a separate sentence.

1 des cheveux
2 des autos
3 des jambes
4 Elles ont

3 In your Activity Book: rewrite the sentences, replacing the words in colour with the words in brackets.

Example:
J'ai *un chat*.   (une grenouille)
J'ai une grenouille.

1 J'ai *des chiens*.   (des chats)
2 Qu'est-ce qu'*il* a?   (elle)
3 *Tu as* des camions.   (J'ai)
4 *Ils* ont les cheveux noirs.   (Elles)
5 Elle n'a pas de *billes*.   (poupées)

Oh! Bélina, tu dessines bien!

Let's learn it in French

When you have finished this unit, you will be able to:
- ask questions and give answers about what people are doing and not doing
- read and write these new words and sentences
- ask and tell the time on the hour

The idea box

Bring the following to class:
- pictures of old castles (you can bring history books, travel books or story books)
- cookies and a broom
- drawings or pictures of houses
- one onion

Situation 1 Tu pleures? Mais non!

Puppets Bélina, Zénon
Props Some onions, a drawing of a house
What happens Zénon is cutting up onions and Bélina comes in to show him her drawing. Though Zénon finds the drawing nice, he sniffles all the time. Bélina asks him why he is sad. Zénon says he is not really crying but just cutting up onions.

Situation 2 Où sont mes biscuits?

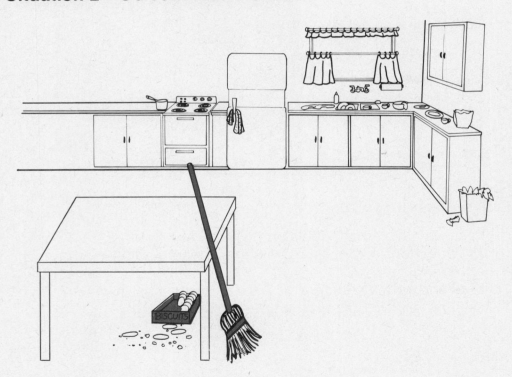

Characters Madame Bonneau, Marc
Setting The Bonneaus' home
What happens Madame Bonneau asks where the cookies she put on the table have gone to. She discovers Marc eating them under the table. She orders him to sweep the floor as punishment, but Marc looks for his ball before starting the job.

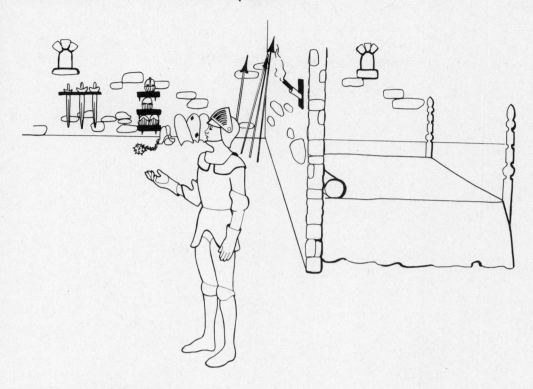

Characters The Lepage family
Setting An old castle
What happens The Lepage family is visiting an old castle. The
spooky castle frightens Nathalie a little, but what she thought was
a ghost is only the tour guide dressed in a suit of armour. In fact,
she even jumps up on an old-fashioned bed. The guide and madame Lepage have to make her get down.

2 Look at the pictures and listen to the sentences. In your Activity Book: write the letter of the sentence that matches each picture.

Ecoute:

Chanson

(Mélodie: Mon beau sapin)

1 Je coupe, je coupe des oignons,
Et cela fait pleurer Zénon.
Il cherche, il cherche son oiseau,
Qui saute sur un vieux chapeau.

2 Je mange, je mange mon gâteau,
Regarde, c'est un beau château.
Tu manges, tu manges ton soldat,
Un beau soldat en chocolat.

La mère de Marc demande: "Tu manges mes biscuits, Marc?"
"Non, dit Marc, je ne mange pas de biscuits. Regarde, Maman, je
cherche ma balle".

Maintenant, il nettoie le plancher.

Nathalie saute sur le lit dans un château. Le guide est très fâché.
"Ne saute pas sur le lit, dit le guide, descends!"

A la maison, Zénon coupe des oignons et Bélina dessine une maison. Mais Zénon ne regarde pas son dessin. Il pleure? Non, il ne pleure pas. Bélina est contente. Elle dit: "Regarde, Zénon, je dessine bien".

1 Ask your friend these questions.

  1 Qu'est-ce que Marc cherche?
  2 Marc nettoie le plancher; c'est vrai?
  3 Nathalie saute sur le lit?
  4 Est-ce que Zénon pleure?
  5 Est-ce que Bélina dessine bien ou mal?

2 Explain that the second person mentioned is not doing what the first person does.

Example:
Je saute sur le lit.   Et Jojo?
Elle ne saute pas sur le lit.

  1 Tu pleures.   Et Zénon?
  2 Je mange une pomme.   Et Filou?
  3 Il nettoie le plancher.   Et madame Bonneau?
  4 Elles cherchent un crayon.   Et Picotin?
  5 Elle dessine.   Et le guide?

3 In your Activity Book: copy these words in the correct order to make a sentence.

  1 saute / elle / lit / sur / le
  2 la / à / maison / vais / je
  3 bien / dessine / je
  4 pomme / une / mange / je
  5 regardent / qu'est-ce qu' / ils

4 In your Activity Book: write the letter of the question that will give the answer.

	Questions to choose from:
1 Je mange une pomme.	a) Qu'est-ce qu'ils nettoient?
2 Marc cherche son chien.	b) Qu'est-ce que Marc cherche?
3 Elles dessinent des fleurs.	c) Qu'est-ce que Nathalie et Jojo dessinent?
4 Oui, tu sautes.	d) Qu'est-ce que tu manges?
5 Ils nettoient la cuisine.	e) Je saute?

unit 14

Quel beau gâteau!

Let's learn it in French

When you have finished this unit, you will be able to:
- ask and tell what you and other people are doing and making
- read and write these new words and sentences
- tell the time on the hour and the half hour

The idea box

Bring the following to class:
- pictures of various cakes
- toys or pictures of various boats and ships
- toys or pictures of houses, dog-kennels, and planes
- a toy clock or an alarm clock

Language of your own

Situation 1   Quel désordre!

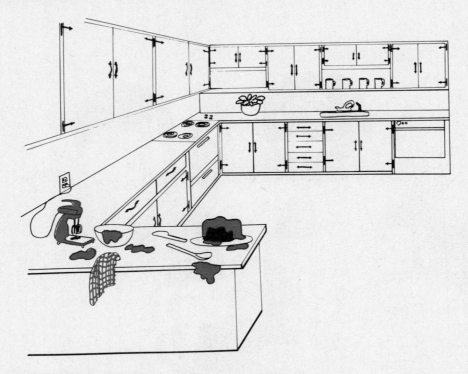

Characters   Monsieur Lepage, Nathalie
Setting   The Lepages' home
What happens   Nathalie is in the kitchen making a cake. The room is in a mess. Monsieur Lepage comes in and sees the mess, but he is not angry with Nathalie, who is so proud of her cake.

Situation 2   Un bateau pour Zénon

Puppets   Picotin, Bélina
Props   A paper boat
What happens   Bélina is making a boat for Zénon. Picotin wants to tell Zénon about it, but Bélina wants it to be a surprise. Picotin agrees to keep quiet, if Bélina will make a boat for him as well.

Characters   The Latulipe family
Setting   The Latulipes' home
What happens   Madame Latulipe hears a lot of noise and asks what is going on. Monsieur Latulipe tells her that Francine and Jules are building another kennel for Filou. Madame Latulipe sits beside the radio and finds that the music is more pleasant to hear.

2 Look at the pictures and listen to the sentences. In your Activity
Book: write the letters (a or b) of the two sentences that match
each picture.

Ecoute:

1

2

Chanson

(Mélodie: Auprès de ma blonde)

Jojo fait un gros gâteau,
Et Nathalie le mange.
Jojo fait un gros gâteau,
Et Nathalie le mange.

Marc et Jules font un bateau,
Et Francine, une niche.

Moi, je fais une cage,
Pour un tout petit oiseau,
Moi, je fais une cage,
Et toi, que fais-tu?

Nathalie fait un gâteau. Quel désordre! Mais son gâteau est beau.
Mmm!

Quelle surprise! Qu'est-ce que tu fais, Bélina? Tu fais un gâteau
aussi? Non, dit Bélina, je fais un bateau pour Zénon. Chut! Chut!
C'est une surprise.

Et qu'est-ce que Jules et Francine font? Une niche pour Filou?
Mais il a une niche! Il saute? Oui, il saute sur sa niche. Quel bruit!

Exercices sur la lecture

1 Look at the sentences and listen to what your teacher reads. In your Activity Book: write the letter of the sentence you hear.

Ecoute:
1 a) Nathalie fait un gâteau.
  b) Nathalie fait un bateau.

2 a) Le bateau de Bélina est une surprise pour Zénon.
  b) Le bateau de Bélina est une surprise pour Picotin.

3 a) Jules et Francine font une niche.
  b) Jules et Francine dansent sur la niche.

4 a) Francine fait du bruit.
  b) Filou fait du bruit.

5 a) Filou a une niche.
  b) Filou a deux niches.

2 In your Activity Book: rewrite the sentences, replacing the words in colour with the words in brackets.

Example:
John pleure. (Il)
Il pleure.

  1 Je fais *une maison*. (un avion)
  2 Tu fais *des niches*. (des biscuits)
  3 *Il* fait une cage. (Elle)
  4 Elles font *une tarte*. (un bateau)
  5 *Tu* fais une niche. (Je)
  6 *Elle* pleure. (Je)
  7 *Nathalie* lance la balle. (Elle)
  8 *Jules et Francine* font une cage. (Ils)
  9 Je fais *un bateau*. (un gâteau)
10 Elle fait *des biscuits*. (une tarte)

unit 15

Où vas-tu?

Let's learn it in French

When you have finished this unit, you will be able to:
- ask where people are going
- understand and give directions
- read and write these new words and sentences
- say how you are
- tell the time on the hour and the quarter hour

The idea box

Bring the following to class:
- toys or pictures of cars, trains, ships, planes
- pictures of cities you have visited or would like to visit
- pictures of a library, a drugstore, a movie theatre, a police station, a bank, a restaurant

Language of your own

Situation 1   Où vas-tu?

Characters   Rosalie, Nathalie
Setting   Rosalie's garden
What happens   Nathalie wants to go to Paris by car. Rosalie bursts out laughing when she hears this. Nathalie, who does not understand that there is an ocean to cross, then decides to go by train to Paris and imitates the sound of a train whistle.

Situation 2   Au revoir, Picotin

Puppets   Zénon, Picotin
Props   A suitcase
What happens   Picotin and Zénon are arguing. Zénon takes his suitcase and announces that he is going to Hong Kong. Picotin does not want his friend to leave and decides to go also. Zénon agrees to stay at home.

Situation 3   Ce n'est pas drôle!

Characters   Jules, monsieur Lepage
Setting   A street
What happens   Jules asks monsieur Lepage how to get to the library when he is right in front of it. Monsieur Lepage plays a trick on him. He tells him to go right around the block. When Jules does not understand, he draws a square in the air with his finger.

2 Look at the pictures and listen to the sentences. In your Activity
Book: write the letter of the sentence that matches each picture.

Ecoute:

1 & 2

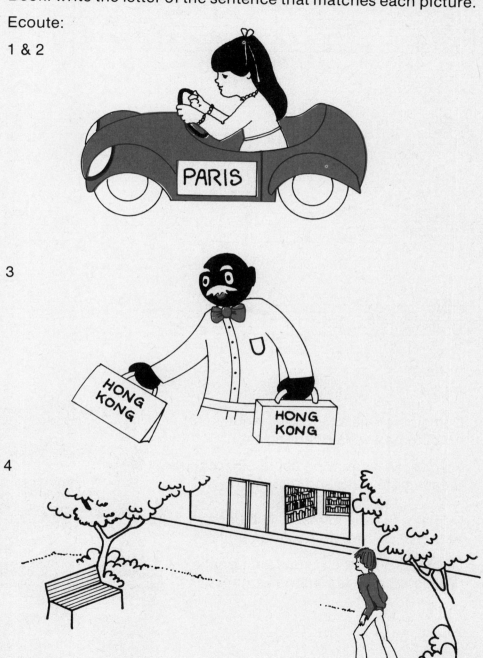

3

4

Chanson

(Mélodie: M'en revenant de la jolie Rochelle)

Refrain

1 Demain, je vais à la bibliothèque,   (2)
   Au cinéma et à la pharmacie.

   Pardon, Monsieur, où est la bibliothèque?
   C'est à côté du grand restaurant.

2 Demain, je vais au restaurant Lepage,   (2)
   Au parc, au zoo, au poste de police.

   Dis Jojo, où est le restaurant Lepage?
   C'est à côté de la banque Bonneau.

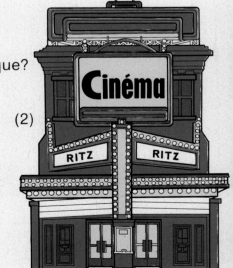

Lecture

1 Marc, où vas-tu?
   Je vais au parc.

2 Zénon ne va pas à Hong Kong.
   Où va-t-il?
   Il va à la bibliothèque.

3 Où est-ce que je vais, Papa?
   Tu vas à la banque, Jojo.

4 Où vont-ils?
   Ils vont à Paris.

5 Francine va au cinéma?
   Non, elle va au restaurant.

6 Rosalie et sa maman vont
   à New York.

⁸² Exercices sur la lecture

1 In your Activity Book: write the letter (a, b or c) of the sentence that is true for the text you have just read.

1 a) Marc va au parc.
  b) Marc va à la bibliothèque.
  c) Marc va à la banque.

2 a) Zénon ne va pas à Hong Kong.
  b) Il va à Hong Kong.
  c) Il va au cinéma.

3 a) Rosalie et sa maman vont à Paris.
  b) Rosalie et sa maman vont à New York.
  c) Rosalie et sa maman vont au restaurant.

2 Look at the sentences and listen to what your teacher reads. In your Activity Book: write the letter (a or b) of the sentence you hear.

1 a) Où sont-ils?
  b) Où vont-ils?

2 a) Ils vont au restaurant.
  b) Ils sont au restaurant.

3 a) J'ai une maison.
  b) Je vais à la maison.

4 a) Où est-ce que je vais?
  b) Qu'est-ce que je fais?

5 a) Zénon ne va pas à Hong Kong.
  b) Zénon va à Hong Kong.

3 In your Activity Book: rewrite the sentences, replacing the words in colour with the words in brackets.

1 *Je vais* au parc.   (Tu vas)
2 Il va à la *bibliothèque*   (maison)
3 *Zénon* ne va pas à Hong Kong.   (Il)
4 *Ils vont* au restaurant.   (Elle va)
5 Où vont-*ils*?   (elles)

Les saisons

The idea box

Bring the following to class:
- objects or pictures which suggest one of the four seasons (for example, a hockey stick, a sun hat, some fruit, leaves of different colours)
- a thermometer
- a calendar printed in French
- an appointment book

Situation C'est l'été

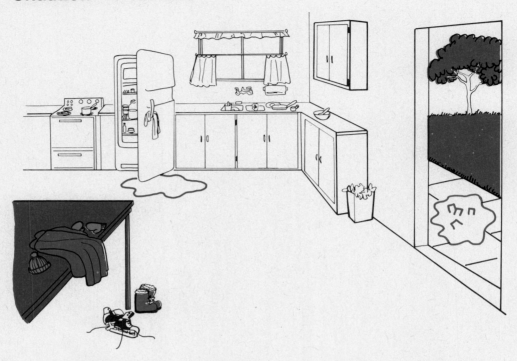

Characters Francine, Marc
Setting The Bonneaus' house
What happens It is summer, the sun is shining. Marc is in the kitchen. He has put his coat, his boots, his hat, his mittens, and his skates on the table. Francine, his babysitter, asks him where he is going. Marc pretends that he is going skating. He has put the ice from the refrigerator outside on the patio. Francine is upset.

Choose your topic II

Joyeux Noël!

The idea box

- In this unit you will make some Christmas decorations and cards.

Language of your own

Situation   Joyeux Noël, Papa!

Characters   Monsieur Lepage, Nathalie, Jojo
Setting   The Lepages' living-room
What happens   It is December 23. Monsieur Lepage is dressed up as Santa Claus. He is practising his Ho! Ho! Ho! in front of a mirror in the living-room. Oh! he has forgotten to put on his boots. Nathalie and Jojo come in, talking. Jojo recognizes her father's slippers but Nathalie pretends that it is Santa Claus.

Voilà c'que le Père Noël

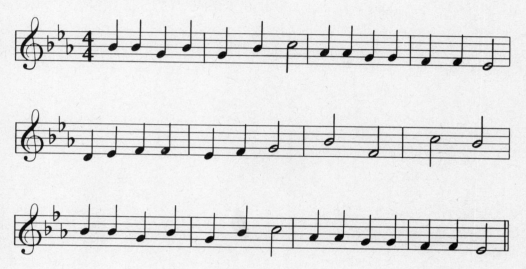

1 Voilà c'que le Père Noël
   M'apporte en cadeau du ciel,
   Un p'tit chien
   Qui fait oua-oua,
   Oua-oua, oua-oua!
   Voilà c'que le Père Noël
   M'apporte en cadeau du ciel.

2 Voilà c'que le Père Noël
   M'apporte en cadeau du ciel,
   Un p'tit chat
   Qui fait miaou,
   Miaou, miaou!
   Voilà c'que le Père Noël
   M'apporte en cadeau du ciel.

Choose your topic III

Joyeuses Pâques!

The idea box

Bring the following to class:
- coloured Easter eggs
- Easter chicks, baskets, rabbits and candies (pictures or objects)

Language of your own

Situation   Où sont les oeufs?

Characters   Jules, Francine
Setting   The Latulipes' house
What happens   Jeannot the rabbit is at Jules' and Francine's house. He is tired out after hiding eggs around the house. When Jules and Francine appear, he hides by jumping on top of the refrigerator.

Vocabulaire

Français – Anglais

Le numéro indique l'unité dans laquelle le mot ou l'expression paraît pour la première fois.

A

a has /11
  il/elle a he/she has /11
à to; in; at; on /2
  à droite on the right; to the right /15
  à gauche on the left; to the left /15
  à la maison at home /10
  à qui est-ce? whose is it? /6
un/une acrobate an acrobat /9
un aéroport an airport /15
ah! oh! /1
ai have /11
  j'ai I have /11
aller to go /15
allez! go! /10
un animal an animal /2
apporte! – apportez! bring! /14
as have /11
  tu as you have /11
assieds-toi! – asseyez-vous! sit down! /2
attrape! – attrapez! catch! /9
  n'attrape pas! – n'attrapez pas! don't catch! /9
au (à + le) to the; in the; at the /2
  au cirque at the circus /9

au marché at the market /5
au zoo at the zoo /2
au revoir goodbye /1
aussi too; also /9
une auto a car /6
autre other /5
un avion an airplane /11
avoir to have /11
  avoir chaud to be warm; to be hot (a person) /11
  avoir faim to be hungry /14
  avoir froid to be cold (a person) /11

B

un balai a broom /13
une balle a ball (small) /3
un ballon a ball (large) /11
une banane a banana /5
une banque a bank /10
un bateau a boat /11
un bâton a stick; a bat /6
beau fine; good-looking; handsome /14
beige beige /3
une bibliothèque a library /15

D

dans in; into; on /5

danser to dance /13

de/d' of; from (also possessive) /5

  d'accord O.K. /5

  de quelle couleur est/sont...?
  what colour is/are...? /11

  de rien you are welcome /5

  pas de/d' not any /11

décrivez-moi describe to me /11

dehors outside /10

demande ask; asks (for) /3

  demande-lui ask him/her /6

  il/elle demande he/she asks /3

demeure live /9

  je demeure à... I live in... /9

une dent a tooth /11

un/une dentiste a dentist /1

derrière behind /10

des some; from the /5

descends! — descendez! come
down! go down! /11

un dessin a drawing /13

dessiner to draw /13

devant in front of /10

une différence a difference /14

un dindon a turkey /2

dis say /5

  tu dis you say /5

disent say /9

  ils/elles disent they say /9

dit says /2

  il/elle dit he/she says /3

un divan a chesterfield; a sofa /3

un docteur a doctor /9

donne-moi give me /3

drôle funny /9

E

une école a school /10

écoute listen (to) /1

un électricien an electrician /1

un éléphant an elephant /2

elle she; it /3

elles they (feminine) /10

en in; by /10

  en auto by car /15

  en bateau by boat /15

  en classe in class /10

  en train by train /15

encore again /13

ennuyeux boring /9

entre! — entrez! go in! come in! /5

es are /5

  tu es you are /5

  tu n'es pas you are not /9

est is /1

  est-ce que (a phrase used to
  begin questions) /10

  il/elle est he/she is /9

  il/elle n'est pas he/she is not /9

et and /2

  et ça? what about that? /2

être to be /9

F

fâché angry /7

la faim hunger /14

  j'ai faim I am hungry /14

faire to do; to make /14

fais do; make /13

  je fais I do; I make /14

  tu fais you do; you make /13

fait does; makes /13

  il/elle fait he/she does; he/she
  makes /13

  il fait chaud it is warm; it is hot
  (weather) /10

  il fait froid it is cold
  (weather) /10

  il fait soleil it is sunny /10

un fantôme a ghost /13

faux wrong /3

ferme! — fermez! close! /6

une ferme a farm /2

un fermier a farmer /1

une fille a girl /1

un film a film; a movie /13

une fleur a flower /5

font do; make /13

94

ils/elles font   they do; they make   /13

froid   cold   /10

   il fait froid   it is cold (weather)   /10

   j'ai froid   I am cold   /11

une fusée   a rocket   /6

G

un garçon   a boy   /1

un gâteau   a cake   /14

gentil/gentille   kind   /10

une girafe   a giraffe   /2

une gomme   an eraser   /7

grand   big; tall   /11

une grenouille   a frog   /5

un/une guide   a guide   /13

H

une heure   an hour; one o'clock   /13

   il est deux heures   it is two o'clock   /13

   il est deux heures et demie   it is half past two   /14

   il est six heures et quart   it is a quarter past six   /15

   quelle heure est-il?   what time is it?   /13

I

ici   here   /15

il   he; it   /3

   il demande   he asks   /3

   il pleut   it is raining   /10

   il y a   there is/are   /5

ils   they (masculine)   /9

intelligent   intelligent   /15

J

une jambe   a leg   /11

un jardin   a garden   /10

jaune   yellow   /3

je/j'   I   /2

   je dors   I am sleeping   /14

   je m'appelle   my name is   /2

   je ne comprends pas   I do not understand   /15

   je ne sais pas   I do not know   /7

joli   pretty   /3

un jongleur   a juggler   /9

un jouet   a toy   /6

une jupe   a skirt   /7

L

la/l'   the (feminine, singular)   /2

là   there   /2

lance! – lancez!   throw!   /9

le/l'   the (masculine, singular)   /5

lentement   slowly   /14

les   the (feminine and masculine, plural)   /5

une lettre   a letter   /11

leur   their   /14

lève-toi! – levez-vous!   get up! stand up!   /2

un lion   a lion   /2

lis! – lisez!   read!   /1

   ne lis pas! – ne lisez pas!   don't read!   /1

un lit   a bed   /3

un livre   a book   /6

M

ma   my (with feminine, singular nouns beginning with a consonant)   /6

madame   Mrs.; madam   /1

mademoiselle   Miss   /1

un magicien   a magician   /9

une main   a hand   /10

maintenant   now   /6

mais   but   /11

une maison   a house   /10

mal   badly   /5

maman mommy /1
manger to eat /13
marcher to walk; to march /13
un martien a Martian /11
mauve mauve; purple /3
un mécanicien a mechanic /1
merci thanks; thank you /5
mes my (with plural nouns) /6
mets! put! /7
mon my (with masculine, singular nouns and singular nouns beginning with a vowel) /6
monsieur Mr.; sir /1
un monstre a monster /11
monter to climb; to go up /2
   monte!—montez! climb! go up! /11
montrer to show /13
   montre-moi show me /3
une motocyclette a motorcycle /11
une moustache a mustache /11

N

un navet a turnip /5
ne . . . pas/n' . . . pas not /1
   ce n'est pas it is not; this is not; these are not /1
   ne lis pas! don't read! /1
nettoyer to clean /13
un nez a nose /11
une niche a kennel /14
noir black /3
non no /1
une nouvelle niche a new kennel /14

O

un oignon an onion /13
ont have /11
   ils/elles ont they have /11
orange orange (colour) /3
une oreille an ear /11
ou or /3
où where /2

où demeures-tu? where do you live? /9
où est . . . ? where is . . . ? /2
où est-il/elle? where is he/she? /10
où sont . . . ? where are . . . ? /7
où vas-tu?—où est-ce que tu vas? where are you going? /15
oui yes /1
ouvre!—ouvrez! open! /6

P

un pantalon a pair of trousers /7
une pantoufle a slipper /7
papa daddy /2
un papier a sheet of paper /14
un parc a park /10
pardon! excuse me! sorry! /10
parler to talk /13
pas de/d' not any /11
petit small; little /2
un pharmacien a druggist; a pharmacist /1
un pied a foot /11
un plancher a floor /13
pleurer to cry; to weep /13
une poire a pear /5
un policier a policeman /11
une pomme an apple /5
une pomme de terre a potato /5
une porte a door /10
un poste de police a police station /15
une poule a hen /2
une poupée a doll /6
pour for /11
pourquoi why /13
prends! take! /7
un professeur a teacher /1

Q

que what; that /2
   que demande . . . ? what does . . . ask? /2

que dit . . . ? what does . . . say? /2
que répond . . . ? what does . . . answer? /5
quel/quelle what; which /3
  de quelle couleur est . . . ? what colour is . . . ? /11
  quel désastre! what a disaster! /3
  quel désordre! what a mess! /14
  quel temps fait-il? what is the weather like? /10
qu'est-ce que what /2
  qu'est-ce que c'est? what is it? /2
  qu'est-ce que tu as? what is the matter? what do you have? /15
  qu'est-ce qu'il y a? what is there? /5
qui who /1
  qui est-ce? who is that? /1
  qui es-tu? who are you? /9
quoi what /2

R

une radio a radio /14
un rectangle a rectangle /3
regarder to look (at) /13
  ne regarde pas! – ne regardez pas! don't look! /3
  regarde! look! /1
  regarde bien look carefully /7
  regardez! look! /10
répond replies; answers /3
  il/elle répond he/she replies; he/she answers /3
réponds reply; answer /5
  qu'est-ce que tu réponds? what do you answer? /5
un restaurant a restaurant /10
reste! – restez! stay! remain! /15
une robe a dress /7
rose pink /3
rouge red /3
une rue a street /13

S

sa his; her; its (with feminine, singular nouns beginning with a consonant) /6
un sac a bag /5
un salon a living-room /5
un sandwich a sandwich /14
sauter to jump /13
ses his; her; its (with plural nouns) /6
s'il te plaît please /5
un singe a monkey /2
un soldat a soldier /13
son his; her; its (with masculine, singular nouns and singular nouns beginning with a vowel) /6
sont are /7
  ils/elles sont they are /10
sors! – sortez! go out! /5
un soulier a shoe /7
sous under /10
un stylo a pen /6
suis am /9
  je ne suis pas I am not /9
  je suis I am /9
sur on /2
une surprise a surprise /5

T

ta your (with feminine, singular nouns beginning with a consonant) /6
une table a table /3
une tarte a pie /14
un téléphone a telephone /11
une télévision a television /11
tes your (with plural nouns) /6
une tête a head /11
ton your (with masculine, singular nouns and singular nouns beginning with a vowel) /6
tourne! – tournez! turn! /15
un train a train /6
un triangle a triangle /3

triste   sad   /15
tu   you   /2
turquoise   turquoise   /3

U

un   a; an (with masculine nouns)   /1
une   a; an (with feminine nouns)   /1

V

va   goes; is going   /14
   il/elle va   he/she goes; he/she is going   /15
   va-t-il?   is he going?   /15
va! – allez!   go!   /10
une vache   a cow   /2
vais   go; am going   /15
   je vais   I go; I am going   /15
une valise   a suitcase   /15
vas   go; are going   /15
   où vas-tu?   where are you

going?   /15
   tu vas   you go; you are going   /15
un ver   a worm   /5
viens ici   come here   /7
un visiteur   a visitor   /13
vite   quick; quickly   /13
voici   here is/are   /13
voilà   there is/are   /3
un voleur   a thief   /11
vont   go; are going   /15
   ils/elles vont   they go; they are going   /15
vrai   right   /3

Y

les yeux   the eyes   /6
   un oeil   an eye   /6

Z

zut!   darn it!   /7

Vocabulary

English — French

The number indicates the unit in which the word or expression appears for the first time.

A

a un/une /1
an acrobat un /une acrobate /9
again encore /13
an airplane un avion /11
an airport un aéroport /15
also aussi /9
am suis /9
  I am je suis /9
an un/une /1
and et /2
angry fâché /7
an animal un animal /2
answer réponds /5
  what do you answer? qu'est-ce que tu réponds? /5
answers répond /3
  he/she answers il/elle repond /3
an apple une pomme /5
are es; sont /5,7
  they are ils/elles sont /10
  where are ...? où sont ...? /7
  you are tu es /5
an arm un bras /11
ask (for) demande /6
  ask him/her demande-lui /6
asks (for) demande /3

he/she asks il/elle demande /3
at à la; à l'; au /2
  at home à la maison /10
  at the circus au cirque /9
  at the market au marché /5
  at the zoo au zoo /2

B

badly mal /5
  things are going badly ça va mal /5
a bag un sac /5
a ball (large) un ballon /11
a ball (small) une balle /3
a banana une banane /5
a bank une banque /10
a bat un bâton /6
to be être /9
a bed un lit /3
behind derrière /10
beige beige /3
a bicycle une bicyclette /11
big grand /11
a biscuit ·un biscuit /13
black noir /3
a blouse une blouse /7

blue bleu /3
a boat un bateau /11
a book un livre /6
boring ennuyeux /9
a box une boîte /5
a boy un garçon /1
bring! apporte! – apportez! /14
a broom un balai /13
but mais /11
by en /15
   by boat en bateau /15
   by car en auto /15
   by train en train /15

C

a cabbage un chou /5
a cage une cage /14
a cake un gâteau /14
a candy un bonbon /10
a car une auto /6
a carrot une carotte /5
a castle un château /13
a cat un chat /2
catch! attrape! – attrapez! /9
a chair une chaise /3
change places changez de
place /3
a chesterfield un divan /3
a chocolate un chocolat /5
a cinema un cinéma /10
a circle un cercle /3
a class une classe /10
a classroom une classe /10
to clean nettoyer /13
to climb monter /2
   climb! monte! – montez! /10
close! ferme! – fermez! /6
a clown un /une clown /9
cold froid /10
   I am cold j'ai froid /11
   it is cold (weather) il fait
   froid /10
a colour une couleur /3
colour! colorie! – coloriez! /3
   colour in . . . colorie en . . . –
   coloriez en . . . /3

come down! descends! –
descendez! /11
come here viens ici /7
come in! entre! – entrez! /5
a cookie un biscuit /13
a cow une vache /2
to cry pleurer /13
to cut couper /13

D

daddy papa /2
to dance danser /13
darn it! zut! /7
a dentist un /une dentiste /1
describe to me décrivez-moi /11
a difference une différence /14
to do faire /14
do fais; font /13
   I do je fais /14
   they do ils/elles font /13
   you do tu fais /13
do not (don't) ne . . . pas/n' . . .
pas /1
   don't catch! n'attrape pas! –
   n'attrapez pas! /9
   I do not understand je ne
   comprends pas /15
a doctor un docteur /9
does fait /13
   he/she does il/elle fait /13
a dog un chien /2
a doll une poupée /6
a door une porte /10
to draw dessiner /13
a drawing un dessin /13
a dress une robe /7
a dresser une commode /3
a druggist un pharmacien /1
a duck un canard /2

E

an ear une oreille /11
to eat manger /13

an electrician un électricien /1
an elephant un éléphant /2
an eraser une gomme /7
excuse me! pardon! /10
the eyes les yeux /6
  an eye un oeil /6

F

a farm une ferme /2
a farmer un fermier /1
a film un film /13
fine beau /14
a floor un plancher /13
a flower une fleur /5
a foot un pied /11
for pour /11
a frog une grenouille /5
funny drôle /9

G

a garden un jardin /10
get up! lève-toi!—levez-vous! /2
a giraffe une girafe /2
a girl une fille /1
give me donne-moi /3
glad content /13
to go aller /15
go vais; vas; vont /15
  I go je vais /15
  they go ils/elles vont /15
  you go tu vas /15
go! va!—allez! /10
go down! descends!—descendez! /11
go in! entre!—entrez! /5
go out! sors!—sortez! /5
go up! monte!—montez! /11
goes va /14
  he/she goes il/elle va /15
  it goes il/elle va /14
good bon /13
good day bonjour /1
good evening bonsoir /1

good-looking beau /14
good morning bonjour /1
goodbye au revoir /1
a guide un/une guide /13

H

the hair les cheveux (m) /11
a hand une main /10
handsome beau /14
happy content /13
has a /11
  he/she has il/elle a /11
a hat un chapeau /7
to have avoir /11
have ai; as; ont /11
  I have j'ai /11
  they have ils/elles ont /11
  you have tu as /11
he il /3
a head une tête /11
a hen une poule /2
her son; sa; ses /6
here ici /15
here is/are voici /13
his son; sa; ses /6
a horse un cheval /2
hot chaud /10
  I am hot j'ai chaud /11
  it is hot (weather) il fait chaud /10
an hour une heure /13
  it is two o'clock il est deux heures /13
a house une maison /10
how comme /13
  how pretty it is! comme c'est joli! /13
how comment /5
  how are things? comment ça va? /5
  how are you? comment vas-tu?—comment allez-vous? /5
how many? combien est-ce que? /11
how much? combien est-ce que? /11

hunger la faim /14
   I am hungry j'ai faim /14
hurray! bravo! /2

I

I je/j' /2
   I am cold j'ai froid /11
   I am hungry j'ai faim /14
   I do not know je ne sais pas /7
   I do not understand je ne comprends pas /15
   I live in . . . je demeure à . . . /9
in à la; à l'; au /10
   in the kitchen à la cuisine /14
   in the restaurant au restaurant /10
in dans /5
   in the box dans la boîte /5
in en /10
   in class en classe /10
in front of devant /10
intelligent intelligent /15
into dans /5
is est /1
   he/she is il/elle est /9
   it is c'est /1
it ce/c' /1
it il/elle /10
   it is a quarter past five il est cinq heures et quart /15
   it is half past two il est deux heures et demie /14
   it is one o'clock il est une heure /13
   it is raining il pleut /10
   it is sunny il fait soleil /10
   it is warm il fait chaud /10
its son; sa; ses /6

J

a juggler un jongleur /9
to jump sauter /13

K

a kennel une niche /14
a key une clé /11
kind gentil/gentille /10
a kitchen une cuisine /13

L

a leg une jambe /11
a letter une lettre /11
a library une bibliothèque /15
a lion un lion /2
listen écoute /1
little petit /2
live demeure /9
   I live in . . . je demeure à . . . /9
a living-room un salon /5
to look (at) regarder /13
   look! regarde! /1
   look! regardez! /10
   look carefully regarde bien /7
to look for chercher /13

M

madam madame /1
a magician un magicien /9
to make faire /14
make fais; font /13
   I make je fais /14
   they make ils/elles font /13
   you make tu fais /13
makes fait /13
   he/she makes il/elle fait /13
a marble (toy) une bille /6
to march marcher /13
a Martian un martien /11
mauve mauve /3
a mechanic un mécanicien /1
mine à moi /6
   it is mine c'est à moi /6
Miss mademoiselle /1
mommy maman /1
a monkey un singe /2
a monster un monstre /11

a motorcycle une motocyclette /11
a mouth une bouche /6
a movie un film /13
a movie theatre un cinéma /10
Mr. monsieur /1
Mrs. madame /1
a mustache une moustache /11
my mon; ma; mes /6
my name is . . . je m'appelle . . . /2

N

a new kennel une nouvelle
niche /14
no non /1
a noise un bruit /14
a nose un nez /11
not ne . . . pas/n' . . . pas /1
  it is not ce n'est pas /1
not any pas de/d' /11
not bad comme ci, comme ça /5
now maintenant /6

O

of de/d' /6
oh! ah! /1
O.K. d'accord /5
on à /15
  on the left à gauche /15
  on the right à droite /15
on dans /13
  on the street dans la rue /13
on sur /2
  on the bed sur le lit /7
an onion un oignon /13
open! ouvre! — ouvrez! /6
or ou /3
orange (colour) orange /3
other autre /5
outside dehors /10

P

a paper (a sheet) un papier /14

a park un parc /10
a pear une poire /5
a pen un stylo /6
a pencil un crayon /3
a pharmacist un pharmacien /1
a pie une tarte /14
a pig un cochon /2
pink rose /3
please s'il te plaît /5
a police station un poste de
police /15
a policeman un policier /11
a potato une pomme de terre /5
pretty joli /3
purple mauve /3
put! mets! — mettez! /7

Q

quack! quack! coin! coin! /2
quick vite /13
quickly vite /13

R

a radio une radio /14
read! lis! — lisez! /1
a rectangle un rectangle /3
red rouge /3
remain! reste! — restez! /15
replies répond /3
  he/she replies il/elle répond /3
reply réponds /5
  what do you reply? qu'est-ce que
tu réponds? /5
a restaurant un restaurant /10
right vrai /3
a rocket une fusée /6

S

sad triste /15
a sandwich un sandwich /14
say dis; disent /5
  I say je dis /5

they say ils/elles disent /9
you say tu dis /5
says dit /3
he/she says il/elle dit /3
a school une école /10
she elle /9
a shirt une chemise /7
a shoe un soulier /7
to shout crier /14
to show montrer /13
show me montre-moi /3
sir monsieur /1
sit down! assieds-toi!—asseyez-vous! /2
a skirt une jupe /7
a slipper une pantoufle /7
slowly lentement /14
small petit /2
so, so comme ci, comme ça /5
a sofa un divan /3
a soldier un soldat /13
some des /5
sorry! pardon! /10
a square un carré /3
ssh! (be quiet) chut! /6
stand up! lève-toi!—levez-vous! /2
stay! reste!—restez! /15
a stick un bâton /6
a street une rue /13
a suitcase une valise /15
a surprise une surprise /5

T

a table une table /3
take! prends! /7
to talk parler /13
tall grand /11
a teacher un professeur /1
a telephone un téléphone /11
a television une télévision /11
thanks; thank you merci /5
that ça /2
what about that? et ça? /2
that ce/c' /1
the le; la; l'; les /2
their leur /14

there là /2
there is/are il y a /5
there is/are voilà /3
these are c'est /6
they (feminine) elles /10
they (masculine) ils /9
a thief un voleur /11
this ce/c' /1
those are c'est /6
throw! lance!—lancez! /9
a tie une cravate /10
to à; à la; à l'; au /2
to the bank à la banque /10
to the left à gauche /15
to the right à droite /15
too aussi /9
a tooth une dent /11
a toy un jouet /6
a train un train /6
a triangle un triangle /3
trousers un pantalon /7
a truck un camion /3
a turkey un dindon /2
turn! tourne!—tournez! /15
a turnip un navet /5
turquoise turquoise /3

U

under sous /10

V

a visitor un visiteur /13

W

to walk marcher /13
warm chaud /10
I am warm j'ai chaud /11
it is warm (weather) il fait chaud /10
to weep pleurer /13

104 **well** bien /5
    things are going well ça va
    bien /5
what comment /2
    what is your name? comment
    t'appelles-tu? /2
what que /2
    what does . . . ask? que
    demande . . . ? /2
what qu'est-ce que /2
    what is it? qu'est-ce que
    c'est? /2
    what is the matter? what do you
    have? qu'est-ce que tu as? /15
    what is there? qu'est-ce
    qu'il y a? /5
what quel/quelle /3
    what a disaster! quel
    désastre! /3
    what a mess! quel désordre! /14
    what colour is . . . ? de quelle
    couleur est . . . ? /11
    what is the weather like? quel
    temps fait-il? /10
    what time is it? quelle heure est-
    il? /13

what quoi /2
where où /2
    where do you live? où demeures-
    tu? /9
    where is . . . ? où est . . . ? /2
which quel/quelle /3
who qui /1
    who are you? qui es-tu? /9
    who is that? qui est-ce? /1
whose à qui /6
    whose is it? à qui est-ce? /6
why pourquoi /13
a wildcat un chat sauvage /2
a worm un ver /5
wrong faux /3

Y

yellow jaune /3
yes oui /1
you tu /2
you are welcome de rien /5
your ton; ta; tes /6
yours à toi /6
    it is yours c'est à toi /6

2 3 4 5 #115900 79 78 77 76